Sheltered
in the Heart

Spirituality in Deep Friendship

Gunilla Norris

Sheltered
in the Heart

Spirituality in Deep Friendship

HOMEBOUND
PUBLICATIONS
Independent Publisher of Contemplative Titles

Homebound Publications books may be purchased for educational, business, or sales promotional use. For information please write:

Homebound Publications Orders Office
Postal Box 1442
Pawcatuck, Connecticut 06379
United States of America

www.homeboundpublications.com
www.gunillanorris.com

FIRST EDITION
ISBN: 978-1-938846-10-6

BOOK DESIGN
Front Cover Image: © Elena Ray (shutterstock.com)
Cover and Interior Design: Leslie M. Browning

10 9 8 7 6 5 4 3 2 1

Homebound Publications holds a fervor for environmental conservation.
Atop donating a percentage of our annual income to an ecological char-
ity, we are ever-mindful of our "carbon footprint". Our books are printed
on paper with chain of custody certification from the Forest Stewardship
Council, Sustainable Forestry Initiative, and the Programme for the En-
dorsement of Forest Certification. This ensures that, in every step of the
process, from the tree to the reader's hands, that the paper our books are
printed on has come from sustainably managed forests.

DEDICATED TO

Stanley, my heart's deep friend

When you love me,
I know me better.
When I love you,
you know you better.
Within the shelter of love
there is no end to knowing.

Contents

Foreword

I am honored--and also wonderfully perplexed--that Gunilla Norris has asked me to contribute the foreword to her luminous new book on spiritual friendship. I am not nearly so confident as she that I will be able to contribute anything to the already exquisite clarity and harmony of her text. I confess to feeling somewhat like a northeasterly gale being invited to blast and rattle my way through a perfectly manicured Japanese garden. I will try my best--big idea person that I am--not to disturb unduly the serenity of the garden.

What Gunilla and I share, beneath some obvious temperamental differences, is our common experience of the path of conscious love--that is, a journey lived deeply and fully with a beloved who is also our closest friend and spiritual companion. It is a path of sheer transparency: grace-filled yet challenging in its complete vulnerability. There is nowhere to hide--for who would want to hide from such a love?--but its radiance also turns up the heat on all those personal evasions and shadow behaviors. It is impossible to claim, "I have been misunderstood!!!" I have been understood only too well, by one who loves me so much that he or she will settle for nothing less than my full emergence into the divine being I was created to be. In the gentle yet relentless crucible of such love, spiritual transformation happens rapidly, as mortal diamonds soon find themselves being ground and polished into "immortal diamonds." For this reason, the path of conscious love—or deep friendship: whichever term speaks more directly to your heart—has been known in the esoteric traditions of the West as "the great cosmic shortcut:" through the solidity of their trust and the integrity of their shadow work, the partners soon burn through their karmic deformations and are free to take their place within the luminous freedom-in-unity that is the true nature of love.

Gunilla writes from this place of luminous freedom. She does not write about the experience of transformed love; she writes from it. She does not gossip or sensationalize; she completely end-runs any drama around finding the perfect partner or how to know whether your particular relationship qualifies as a "deep friendship." That's not what this book is about. She even manages, in a wonderfully sly way, to sidestep the whole question of whether the deep friendship needs to be an erotic partnership at all; her gate is wide open to all manner of friendships—gay, straight, celibate, conjugal, filial, imaginal (and I suppose even with pets and houseplants), so long as they are marked by those foundational qualities of stability, transparency, and openness to spiritual growth.

Instead of giving us criteria for measuring and assessing whether our particular friendship qualifies as "deep," she simply assumes that your heart will recognize the real thing if it's on your plate. Sparing no more time on the diagnostics, she instead leads you across the threshold into her real topic: the spiritual attitudes and practices that attend such deep friendships and emerge as the mature fruits of a life lived in such intimate give-and-take. Each of the short chapters in this book is a profound mediation—etched with Gunilla's signature haiku delicacy—on the spiritual qualities that both guide the skillful stewardship of such a friendship and emerge over time as its most precious gifts. The qualities she addresses—faithfulness, honesty, compassion, self-acceptance, to name only a few—are of course the fruits of any mature spiritual life; but when cultivated along the pathway of intimate friendship, they bear a particular sweetness. Gunilla knows this pathway well—clearly, she has fully integrated the gifts of which she speaks—and her words are a luminous comfort (as well as wise practical advice) for those of us stumbling our way toward maturity in her footsteps. As I read each meditation—pausing and reflecting as she's requested—I found myself reliving my own relational path, savoring those truths I'd come to discover on my own (mostly through trial and error), and wishing I'd had this book in my hands twenty years ago. It would have allowed me to move so much more confidently and serenely in the direction that love was beckoning.

True lovers, Rilke observes in his *Letters to a Young Poet*, are "two silences that border, protect, and salute one another." To my mind, that quote quintessentially captures the spirit of Gunilla's book, and her wise and compassionate reflections beautifully convey the music of this dance. Her book will be a blessing to all who have begun to discover that spaciousness and intimacy are not opposites; they are the warp and weft of a tapestry whose fullness is Love itself.

--Cynthia Bourgeault

Introduction

To have a deep friend is daring, creative, transformative and humbling. It requires focus, dedication, self-giving and two conscious people attending to the movement of love in the depth of their being. In other words it is a spiritual matter.

Casual friends are people we care about, enjoy and do things with. We may have many interests in common with such friends. This is true of deeper friendships, too, but in my experience these friendships have another dimension. They ask us to develop our essence and to grow spiritually. That is something an ordinary friendship might not ask of us.

Based on mutual caring, connection to spirit and a necessity to grow in consciousness the love between friends is a different kind of love than we think of ordinarily. It has freedom in it. It comes and goes by laws of its own and has no guarantees. It requires loving awareness and presence. Above all it is a tender gift that we must live in order to realize.

This book is a collection of reflections culled from many years of dwelling in and caring about this subject. Words will ultimately fail, for deep, spiritual friendship is an experience that contains more than can be articulated. Yet I want to trust that these reflections will bring the reader to examine what it is to have and to be a true friend.

I hope the reader will feel this book to be an invitation, a kind of heart to heart conversation that invites us to be open, to consider matters of the most inward kind. I bring up qualities, activities and attitudes that are helpful in cultivating a deep friendship. As I was writing I found that an afterthought would come to me. These thoughts are printed in italics to invite a slower pace and a encouragement to reverie. I hope you will mull things over and think about what you have read since your response is integral to this conversation.

I use the words God, Spirit, Love, Life and Reality to point to the numinous Unknown in which we live and more and have our being. We know that no name can ultimately describe the Mystery at the heart of all that is. Yet we can have experiences through deep friendship in which we sense how we belong to that Mystery and therefore to everything. Please do not read this book straight through. Let there be time to consider what you would like to add or take exception to. Making space for reflection is often forgotten in our fast paced society. Let's reclaim the leisure to respond from reverie rather than from rushing.

A loving spiritual connection between people is full of nurturing and waiting. It has to take place over time. It is in duration that trust comes into being. As we witness one another's inner beauty and essence we are giving and receiving the greatest of gifts. I hope that in reading this book you will find some useful ideas. I hope you will feel encouraged to draw closer to the ground of your own being and to the growth of your spirit. I hope you might give this book to a special person who is, or might be trusted to be, a true companion on the way.

We are embedded in Mystery of Love. I believe we are asked to develop deep friendships not only for our own sakes but also for the sake of one another and for the sake of Love itself. Together we can attend to the longing that dwells at the core in each and every one of us and so become more of who we essentially are ...parts of Love itself.

--Gunilla Norris
Mystic, CT 2013

Meeting

When we encounter someone who belongs to our soul's journey it will happen in an ordinary way and often in a context we are familiar with. Yet it will also happen in a far larger context. Putting words to this is hard because those larger dimensions are so interwoven with our daytime awareness they are hard to separate out. Yet we sense that something significant is happening to us. There is an excitement in the air. We have a sense even if it is obscure that we have been found. Something has begun that is vital.

Without words we seem to know this. Over time we will discover how we meet in being, in time, in place, in potential and in willingness. Overtime we will savor the joys of deep friendship.

Being

To have a deep friend is to have very special support—yet not as we usually think of support. Such a friend is not a crutch. Such a friend is not someone who will do the inner work we ourselves refuse to do, nor is it someone we hang on to out of loneliness or other unexamined reasons.

Our friend is not to be thought of as either more wise than ourselves nor less wise than we are. We are both unique and equal. As such we are not to use one another. The simple fact that our friend exists at all and is walking his or her path beside us confirms that we are alive in a more than a mundane way. We have a chance to honor the sanctity in each other.

Sometimes it is possible to be with another person without our usual protective layers. We can be natural in a creature-to-creature way. This is a bit like walking in a wood and suddenly coming upon a deer in a glade. Our eyes meet. Our ears prick up. We are exquisitely alert. A special kind of recognition happens. When the deer does not run away, is not frightened, but stays of its own accord on its own business, trusting us and itself to be safe, we feel given to and somehow enlarged. Our natural innocence becomes real. Together we are brought into the purity of simple being. In this light we are simultaneously lifted and illumined.

When two people can be innocent with one another this way it is support of a special kind. It allows us to remember that there is within us, at the very core, a sheer and wild perfection.

ॐ

As deep friends we shelter the transparent beauty we each are. We protect and value one another in the way an endangered species is valued and protected. In recognizing the sheer and wild perfection in one another we understand each other as holy and as free. There will never be another you. There will never be another me.

Time

If the purity of being is the first place that we meet, then time could be considered the second place. Without convergence how could we find each other? We must meet one another at a specific time. It could happen on a Tuesday in early Fall in a particular calendar year. It could be Saturday in spring, two years earlier. It will always be an un-repeatable moment and yet, because being is holy, it will also be a timeless moment. We meet simultaneously in infinity and on Tuesday. Feeling and knowing eternity as always with us brings our shared events into the present and into vastness.

Simple things can be experienced as multi-layered. Take, for instance, having tea together. The warm vapor from the cups floats up, smoking and curling in the air. It is soundless—a melody. Can we sense that we are sipping from the steaming cup of now in the home of forever? The mystery is that in this bit of time when we meet, we also meet everything else.

How much will we be able to drink this in? A sip here and there, and fleetingly at first, but over time and with practice we can taste both worlds at once and drink our fill. We will know we are timelessly in time.

჻

No moment of love is ever lost. Trusting that to be true, we would know that nothing real ever disappears though it changes and continues in some other way. We can't fathom precisely how this is, yet we can trust that it is.

We may be afraid to love because we fear the loss of that love in the future. But are we not both lost and found within the moment's consecration? We are lost because we forget ourselves when we are fully engaged, and we are found again and again in one another's presence.

Living the rich duality of timeliness and timelessness we become spacious and open. Slowly and with practice we can come to feel how inclusive and luminous is Now and how radiant is Always.

Place

The third way we meet is in the sanctity of place. The Zen saying that no snowflake falls into the wrong place gives us a sound perspective.

Wherever we have tumbled to is a right place, despite our propensity to want somewhere better, safer, more exciting, lovelier, and so on. This is especially true when where we are is a cruel and life-threatening situation. Yet even there, given a strong connection to Spirit, we might be able to see our circumstances as part of holy ground.

This is easy to write and searing to live. We meet in being, in time, and in place. The situations we are in color our experiences very much. A deep friend can be met on a train, in the work place, on vacation, in a bank or a barrack. We belong to places even if those places are transient. We cannot be together unless we converge in place and in time.

Now with the Internet a friend can be met in a placeless place, a virtual space. But sooner or later we will want to find our friend in the solidity of an actual location. Being human we need to touch one another, to come together in more than imagination, thought or word.

To meet in the sanctity of place is to honor that we each must have room to be. Our bodies take up space. We are always in a specific somewhere. Wherever that happens to be, it is always a here. It is in place that we can feel that we are of earth and in mutual connection. It is there that we know we are in the universe and have the universe within us.

ରୀ

When we meet at the crossroad, under the clock, at the train or by the big oak in the park, we are there solidly as we physically are. Yet we are there in a far bigger way than we know.

Whatever our actual size we have an inner space that is immense. There is no way we can be mapped. So why not think of our heart's friend as an expanding universe? Would we not then sense that we are vast as well?

It is a joy to see the stars in one another.

Potential

There is another place where we meet. It is in the realm of potential. When two people truly meet, immediately something new has happened. We see this easily with children. The moment they have each other's measure and feel a bit secure, they begin to create together both known games and new ones as chance will have it.

As adults haven't we experienced a sense of empowerment with someone we have affinity with? We are awakened to play and to discover. It is as natural as breathing. Brought close to one another, two smoldering logs in a fireplace catch heat from one another and begin to burn more brightly. An existing and vital potential is brought out in both. The energy is evident. Whenever we sense capacity in another we are natural catalysts and become agents of encouragement. This is always the case when we are lucky to find someone who resonates with our being.

How wonderful it is then to look upon one another as catalysts of inspiration and potential. This way of seeing can become a habit of welcome, a great courtesy of heart. And when we are also perceived this way, there is a new lightness to our step, a sense of possibility that supports us.

ॐ

It is good to know that to be a true friend of even one person is a lifetime's opportunity. The heart's journey is too deep to share with more than a very few. Such a chance may be rare, but when it comes a fire starts in which much is forged.

We are ignited, tempered and warmed. We see the world with new eyes and are born—birthed and carried along into what we have the potential to become.

Willingness

nother inexplicable meeting place is in the attitude of willingness--that convergence of instinct and feeling. Why we are willing to be suddenly and freely open to another human being is a complete mystery. The people we travel in depth with can be so different from our usual connections. Why the heart simply says yes, we will not know. But could we not suspect that such openings are not chance but Spirit at work--that we are brought together for a reason beyond mere liking or curiosity? Are we not to form something, to become something in association with that other, who is precisely the one who needs us as we need them?

Such travel companions do not have to be companions for life, though they can become that. They are not necessarily our spouses or our best friends. As companions on the way they enter our journey with significance, and our hearts are flung open.

When we think of the most important events of our lives they are usually not constructed. They happen in a moment, in a place, out of simply being who we are. In the excitement of recognition we say, Yes. This yes is not from the mind but from a place that lies beyond our ken. Could we say that we enter into a kind of response—ability to and for one another? It is as if we were mysteriously brought to a trailhead to begin a journey. We do not know where the path may lead; only that Spirit has opened a way for us both.

ଅଅ

We usually sense affinity at once, but it can also happen with someone we initially have little in common with, who in time is revealed to be a deep friend. The fact dawns on us slowly. Many small events are needed before a match is struck and we find our hearts kindled.

Moments of knowing can never be planned. They are given to us. Our responding "yes" is given to us as well. We cannot force it. We can only recognize it and then gratefully receive it.

Such a response is spontaneous—a gift and an opening. We know we are living a significant and fiery moment.

Understanding

How much we long to be understood. Fundamentally this is not about being in agreement though that seems to make things appear easier. But understanding is much deeper than that. It is a profound spaciousness that grants another person the chance to be known from their own perspective and revealed in their history, their joys, their sorrows, their struggles and strengths.

When we really understand one another that way it is like making a beautiful ring of support. The jewel of the self is given a setting in which to be held and seen. It is one of the dearest parts of friendship.

The Past

When we embrace the sanctity in each other we have a foundation on which much can be built. We naturally want to understand more about what has made us who we are. That is the stuff of intimacy. It deepens and enlarges our connection.

Does it matter that our friend knows where we were born, what our family was like, what schools we attended, what places we lived in, who we loved in the past? The answer is, no. We do not need to know these things to feel and honor the sanctity in one another.

Yet even casual friends want to know a little about each other. It is natural in a friend to know many of these particulars. In a deep friendship such things are important but not in a classifying way. Our histories have shaped us, but we are not defined by them.

We don't want to know things about each other in order to categorize, summarize or define one another. Knowing each other's past is simply background. The foreground is our moment-to-moment experience.

Taking distance from our past we are like birds flying over a terrain. We can feel the thermals rising from the territory of the past. We are warmed and lifted by some of them, and some suck us down. Strong wings are needed to bear up. Side by side we help gain perspective and understanding. It is very hard to observe our selves clearly on our own. Without a loving other it is almost impossible to know who we are.

෨෨

Sharing our past is a sacred trust. It is not casual. In a deep friendship we can trust that our histories will never be used against us. When we remember together we actually reconstruct the body of our past. We gain perspective and often reassurance.

We also discover unresolved pain, and it is not so much what happened to us that is as important as how we responded to what happened. Our histories carry the facts, but it is how we experienced those facts, and what we did with them, that will reveal who we really are.

Giving each other heartfelt acceptance opens us to more self-acceptance.

Joys

Revisiting the past is a bit like looking at a marked map. We know the sequence of where and when things happened. We can trace the path we once traveled. But entering the realm of memory we will no longer be *above* events, we will be *in* them. Recollection allows us to re-experience. Memories are often changed a bit when we share them with someone we trust.

Together we open to more knowing and feeling. For some, sharing past joy is more poignant than sharing past pain. When we recall the joys of our early life we are no longer looking at a map, we are in the territory of experience. We are both living *now* and re-living *then*, and have access to our youthful sense of things, the vivid *such-ness* of the world.

The taste, smell, and touch of goodness, when shared with another, will be present once again. In our friend's eyes we will know, not only that joy happened to us, but that the capacity for it is still alive and well in us. For each of us there is a pattern to that which consistently gives us joy

Early joys are very powerful. We know what

touched us though we can't explain the sense of kin-
ship with it. Nurtured, planted and given roots, early
joys are soul-seeds that remain alive in us until the end
of our lives.

∾

*Though we might not easily remember, something germane
continues from our early years—a wonder, a knowing, a
particular way to fall in love with the world.*

*When we know something about that we can further
one another. Remembering and cultivating joy is not frivo-
lous. It is a spiritual fire which when it burns can bring us
into our true work in the world.*

*With a loving friend we can discover early seeds of joy
that still guide our choices in life, and if these joys are not yet
lived we can help each other to bring them into life so that
we can embody them.*

*Joy is a mark of the Spirit. We express joy when we live
what allows us to feel who we essentially are.*

Sorrows

Whenever we remember our joys we cannot help but remember our sorrows as well. They are tied together. When we remember the one, the other seems also to be pulled out of the past into present awareness. This is so because by its nature joy includes all that is not yet within its compass.

Inner joy unlike happiness is not dependent on circumstance. It is a condition of being--a profound acceptance of pathos. Could we dare to say that joy is not joy unless sorrow has found a home within it? That can change how we look upon our grief. Accepted, it becomes the royal road to that transcendent place of knowing life as it really is--sweet, bitter and true. Sorrows refine us. Embracing them our souls grow. The dross is burned out of us when we submit to the fire. As the alloys--our preferences and insistences--melt away, we can begin to feel how everything, even dreadful things can carry meaning and forge us into wholeness.

Sharing one another's sorrows is a tender aspect of deep friendship. We should not be so ready to be rid of our grief when it is the very path to the heart. Together we realize that sorrows fully accepted mark our faces. We seem to shine with wisdom when we are able to witness this in each other. We acknowledge a sense of wholeness, a realized strength in our bearing.

∞

Whenever any sorrow is taken fully to heart we learn something profound. A window opens where a door closed. The soul expands. Assumptions about ourselves are shed. We become naked to actual experience, and therefore more joined to the world.

We know how easy it is to fall into self-pity or into pity for another. But the loving thing is to see one another as being capable of whatever comes our way. If we do not refuse our sorrows and kiss them instead, will they not become beautiful? Wouldn't the world glitter through our tears as the sun does after rain?

Struggles

There are forces that defeat us, perhaps must defeat us, so that we can somehow become truer persons. Could we think of these challenges as angels we must wrestle with until we gain a blessing from them as Jacob did in the Old Testament? Deep friends can help each other here. We want to complain when things are tough, and we strategize to overcome whatever is in our way. But if we could ask each other what the inherent blessing is in what is difficult we would be better served.

Not for a moment are we to skirt over the grit, sweat and pain of challenges, but we can see them as other than useless pain. If we could consider them somehow as worthy forces, then our struggles with them would have dignity. We might lose many battles, but we would not lose our connection to Spirit. How would we know anything about our selves without such angels? Wouldn't we remain untested, untried and somehow never reach spiritual maturity?

Tests in life inevitably come. If we wallow in our difficulties and use our precious energy in complaint we merely become victims. If we grin and bear them or deny our challenges we are numbed. If we are fighting someone else's battle we often rob them of their chance for resolution and dignity. It is only when the challenge is truly ours, and when we give our all, that both victory and defeat become less important. It is then we are asking for a blessing and not an outcome.

ဢ

As we share when and how we have suffered, could we listen without pity? Could we help each other and not enable each other, taking the time to consider what is truly of help? Let us not assume we know for a fact.

With patience we lend our presence as our friend grapples. Tempted to intervene we can remember that the struggle belongs to our friend and is not ours. This is true in reverse. We must trust each other to be capable of wrestling with our angels.

To trust this way is reverent. Misguided help can be worse than no help. Let us be the help that supports both dignity and endurance.

Strengths

Struggles seem to be matched with strengths the way joy is matched with sorrow. We are not tested everywhere. Our struggles are usually particular to our character. When we are able to meet our difficulties without shirking, we become more of who we really are. There is a curious mercy here for we usually do not get more than we can bear. And when we bear whatever we must to its fullest, to term, we give birth to something new in ourselves -- a larger capacity of being.

Strength is often thought of as might, endurance or some form of force. But spiritually speaking, strength is the great art of not fighting against what is but engaging it will all our heart. Sometimes that amounts to a forti-tude that allows things to be or to develop without our insistence. Perhaps inner strength is a kind of mother love. It holds difficulty like a baby and looks for what is needed rather than for what is wanted. Held in such tender awareness we are also held back from precipitous action.

When we understand our lives better, we can see where such strength was at work. Always a gift given by Spirit, it is a surprise to us that we were able to prevail.

Is it not often after the fact that we discover we have been given the gift of strength?

A true friend can give us encouragement by knowing our history, our joys and our sorrows, our struggles and our strengths, and in their eyes we can see ourselves better.

ಬಬ

What one person carries easily another person cannot bear. We join strength with strength. A single stick is easily broken. Two sticks together are harder to snap. Together we bear our own and each other's burdens better, and we understand when the other must go it alone.

Sometimes holding is simply the ability to see a bigger picture. Sometimes holding is support and nurturing help, and sometimes holding is holding back and letting things be. In retrospect the latter is often sensed as profound help though in the present we might feel it as counter intuitive. We are, after all, still present for one another though we are not "doing anything".

Deep friends know they are trusted to handle their own challenges in their own way and in their own timing.

Honesty

The mind has many tricks. It can fool us. On the one hand we can name what we believe to be true while on the other hand we can hide what we are ashamed of or not capable of facing at a given time. It is not uncommon to make separate compartments for different aspects of our actions and thoughts. Even to be aware that we have denials takes great courage.

Honesty requires much emotional nakedness and vulnerability. In contrast to the mind, a loving heart has a greater capacity to hold our shadow or our unformed knowing. The witness that a friend brings to us with such a heart can help us in the great work of becoming true to ourselves for together we can gain clarity, sort priorities, face our faults,understand the vows we have made and keep to our devotion.

Clarity

Understanding the issues we each grapple with, we help each other gain clarity. No problems are solved until they are identified. No goals are reached until they are named. Within a relationship of trust and love we have the assurance of honesty and the generosity of presence that helps us sort things out.

Everyone faces challenges and issues--those places where decisions are made and character is revealed. Identifying what is going on at any given time is a first step. It requires that we love one another not only with our hearts but with our minds also. In the midst of an issue we might not know what is happening. As we clarify there is a sifting that goes on--a bit like using a sieve at the beach. There is always so much extraneous stuff that must pass through for us to be able to see the stones that block the flow--the stumbling blocks at the bottom of it all.

Together we can let the sand run and see what remains. Clarifying what is in the way of our path is a form of mutual intercession. When we try to do this alone we often have doubts and tend to second-guess our selves. Together we create a stronger knowing of the truth and gain the confidence that though we do not yet have solutions, we are making clear what belongs to us to deal with. Isn't wisdom often just this — the patience to allow for extraneous issues to empty out and so reveal what is left for us to face and deal with?

ༀ

How we sort colors our future solutions.

Identifying things in fear or judgment makes those things our enemies. Clarifying them as mere facts of life may be pragmatic but may also lack feeling. Naming with spunk, naming with humor—all color our future solutions.

Could we not only learn to be honest about our issues, but also realize how we sense and feel them? This brings us into a fuller knowledge of the tasks before us and what can be changed for the better.

An issue may not be so daunting in and of itself. The difficulty may lie in how we think and feel about it. When we are able to tease each other or encourage each other it is as if we put a tinted gel over a spotlight. The stage we then see goes from something drab and dark to a more colorful set where new acts can begin.

Priorities

When beset by whatever challenges us, we not only have to be honest about the problem and our attitude towards it, but we must also set priorities for handling both the circumstance and the feelings we have. We might ask: *What is most chronic? What must be handled first? Can it be handled first?* Helping one another to set goals and priorities is like making a trip-tick for a journey.

We may not know entirely where we want to go, or must go, but we have at least clarified where we are. In doing so we have opened the possibility of traveling several roads. Sometimes it may be that the priority we come to is no action at all--just days of needed rest or time for the *nothing* we never allow ourselves.

In a deep friendship where one of us cannot see what the priority is, the other is often able to do so. Where one of us is still pushing the gas pedal, the other may know to steer us into a rest stop. Our heart's friend may also be able to see that we cannot do something alone or should not.

There are so many things that determine where we find ourselves. So many roads have converged to the specific spot on our life's map where we happen to be now. It's there we have an opportunity to decide what we are about, what must be left behind, what must be left dormant and what, even very small thing, can change the whole nature of our journey. Helping each other set priorities is a huge mutual gift.

∽∾∽

We travel together in so many ways and we may even arrive at the same destination, but we have different ways to order what is important to each of us. To share our priorities when neither of us is in stress or distress is a wonderful thing. We learn how we order those things that are important to us just for the fun of knowing.

Then, if we are ever in an urgent moment of having to choose, we will be able to remind each other of what matters most to each.

Having a deep friendship can be a priority in and of itself, though there will be times when we cannot act on it. Still we can feel that we are there with each other and for each other.

We can accept that our heart's friend must sometimes take a road away from us until it is possible to come together again.

Faults

To be honest about our faults in the presence of love takes guts and humility. It is healing to name our failings and unhelpful habits of being. It is important to have no illusions about our selves either in detriment or in self-assigned grandeur. We are so very human, of the earth--a kind of humus, and from a larger perspective, very humorous, too. Really, how important do we think we are?

When the friend of our heart still loves us despite our worst faults, we can learn to love ourselves better. To be revealed with the limps of character we each have is very naked, indeed. This is the humus we must work with all our lives most likely. We may improve a little, but the tendencies to anger, impatience, discouragement, grandiosity, delusion, lack of courage etc. etc. are there, mixed in with our positive qualities.

Perhaps we are born with these inherent tendencies. Perhaps our intrinsic goodness and our innate faults are meant to meet day by day in order to compost into something organic and vital? Then who would we most want to have in our corner if not our heart's friend who honors the whole process with us? Who, but our friend, will be our sometime catalyst, confidant, challenger, confessor and consoler?

ಬಬ

In a museum any bronze statue with an unusual body part, such as a big nose or a humpback, seems to get touched. Hand after hand strokes the nose, the back, and the giant toe. It is uncanny how these symbolic faults are recognized. We touch them in an unconscious acknowledgement that we all have faults even if they are internal and not on display.

No museum guard is fast enough to stop these quick caresses. Little by little the metal starts to lighten up, and in time it begins to glisten.

Could it be that in recognizing and caressing the unwanted truth, new light comes through--in fact, must come through?

Vows

I t can be easier to be honest about our goals and priorities than to be honest about our vows. Vows are a different order of commitment. We don't state priorities when we marry, enter a religious order, or commit our lives to something for the long haul. We take vows. They are of a greater magnitude. We take them in front of others to be witnessed by them and to have their support. We know a vow needs to be made with our whole being, for once decided upon and witnessed, our lives will be profoundly changed. It is a promise given to our selves and to Spirit.

A vow can be thought of as a spine. It holds us up. It holds us together. To break it is to break apart. To make a vow is to name the commitment to something or to someone and to the loneliness such a commitment entails. Vows are up to us to keep. No one can live them for us.

Sometimes we do not know that we have taken a vow. It is secret, unwitnessed and hidden in our unconscious. *I will never again...or I must always...* We made vows such as these when we were vulnerable and immature.

Such vows are often made not to be *for* something, but to protect us from a future hurt. Hidden vows are sometimes the ones that prevent us from making the life giving ones that complete and fulfill us.

ตออ

As deep friends could we uncover the vows that are unconscious and detrimental in our lives? Together we might then also find the new vows we can make, the ones that bring us into full personhood.

As deep friends we see how we live and so can ask those questions that cause us to be more and more truthful. Are we living with and for our vows? Can we be honest about what matters to us? Without mutual witnessing we may not ever come to know what we are living for. In a vow it seems that bliss and challenge are always paired. Do we accept them both?

Challenged—-our backs to the wall—-we are stretched to the utmost for the sake of our heart's promise. We suffer it and often that very suffering is the portal to meaning and to our bliss.

There is a loneliness imbedded in the making and the keeping of a vow. As we live our dedication, we witness each other's existential aloneness. Because that is a shared human truth it helps keep our spines erect.

We back each other up.

Devotion

Could we honestly name what we worship? Who is God for us? We know God cannot in reality be named, for naming, even as it reveals also conceals. The Mystery that is God has no limits and cannot be defined. And yet we know the profound human need to call God by name. The names of God are continually and infinitely revealed and revered in countless ways: Spirit, Companion, Love, Justice, Peace, Grace, Fruition, Beauty, Redemption, Forgiveness—on and on goes the naming as aspects of God become numinous for us.

What name of God is central to us? Being honest about how God touches us we can better worship together. If we understand our friend's devotion to an aspect of God, we can honor it and be honored in return.

Many traditions chant a sacred name in relation to an aspect of God. What name would sing in our hearts and call us to daily remembrance? This may change at different times in our lives. Where Justice might once have been the name we felt most drawn to in our relationship to God, it may be that Mercy becomes what we grow into in later years.

This can be a fierce territory. We know dreadful wars have been fought over which name is the true and only name for God. Could we remember that at the core in each of us is God, the un-namable Presence who whispers our name in a still small voice? That name is for us to hear. It is for us to become.

ॐ

We worship gods we do not recognize as such. They are hidden. We respond to them automatically, compelled somehow to turn towards them in devotion. Addictions are like that whether to substances, activities, or habits of thought and emotional leanings.

Once triggered, we give ourselves to these inauthentic gods looking for something to shield us from fear, uncertainty or boredom.

Could we be honest about what enslaves us? In doing so we might be able to stop our unconscious devotion to illusory gods and turn instead to the One in whom we really live and move and have our being.

With clarity about our faults, our priorities, our vows and our devotion could we come to know that we are already in the awesome mystery of God's love where we are called by name?

Faithfulness

Faithfulness requires presence and awareness more than we might ever think. It is not static, a one-time decision we make. Faithfulness is a continuous process with daily attendance and care. It requires that we grow beyond the present moment because life will inevitably bring us tensions and conflicts to address. We will have to declare where we say yes and where we must draw a line and say no. To be faithful we must discriminate and adhere to our deepest intuitions and commitments.

Not only in our quiet, contemplative times when we intercede for one another, but also in the hubbub of daily activities faithfulness is a lived prayer. It demands that we become trustworthy for the sake of our heart's dear friend and for the depth of our being.

Tension

A profound characteristic of a deep friendship is that it is faithful. This means a quality of presence that can be counted on over time. It means an innocence of heart that remains open even in difficulty. It means a trust that whatever befalls us; our friendship can be understood to be about mutual development. In the marriage ceremony we say *for better or for worse*. In a consecrated friendship we might say *in trust that Spirit is taking us deeper into life*.

Faithfulness is a virtue that can tolerate disappointment and difficulty. It makes us human persons instead of mere individuals. Faithfulness is not some kind of blind acquiescence and acceptance of one another. Faithfulness has muscle. It has duality built into it for we need to be faithful to our own inner truth as well as to support the truth of our friend. This may challenge us to be true in opposite directions. In that tension the new in both of us can be born.

The ability to bear tension with vigor and equanimity is what makes music of relatedness. Think of a guitar and how its strings must be fastened at two ends and must be strung to a bearing pitch. It is only possible in that condition to play the instrument and to sound a true note. In a deep friendship we cannot escape that our hearts have to be tuned frequently. We will be asked to confront one another at times, to say *yes* and *no* clearly and to love each other through conflicting desires.

∞

On the one hand, we lean into and trust the faithfulness of our special friend. On the other hand, we attend to our mutual commitment as if it needed constant tuning. What a paradox! Trust and watchful attentiveness —it seems they would cancel each other out.
A dual aspect of a muscle is that it contracts and expands. Like any muscle, faithfulness can only lift and carry if it is used. Contracting and expanding we learn the mysteries of deep companionship. Then, whatever of inner growth happens belongs to us both.

Saying No

Spiritual friends do not enable one another--we ennoble each other instead. There is genuine carefulness in our interactions, and because that is true, it is more vital that we are able to say no. This can seem counter-intuitive.

Let's suppose that we have conflicting desires in a given moment. One of us needs the other to be available for talk and comfort, and the other needs at the very same moment to be alone. How does one say no either to one's own desire or to the desire of the other? It requires that we feel the tension, and that we refuse to go into an automatic response. Could we ask what would ennoble the relationship--what would honor the tensile strength of it? We can only find out by finding out. If we can pause long enough to feel the heart's capacity to hold disparate things, we would say our no's in such a way that we do not reject the other--or feel rejected by the other--and remain in our integrity.

Then we embrace the whole of the situation, not just our own particular part of it. We say our no's from a stretched heart. A gentle no is so much more loving than an acquiescing yes. We will feel the considerations that go into the answers we give. We can feel the honoring of both self and other and the trust we have in our friend not to take offense.

There may be many times we might feel disappointed by each other's no's, but that is far different from experiencing rejection.

ॐ

We can practice saying no. *There are many moments available for a kind* no. *If we practice when we are apart from our friend, our comfort with* no *might get easier. We may begin by smiling at habits we want to change and say a loving* no *to them.*

Perhaps this could be no *to a second helping of food or* no *to avoiding doing the taxes, or* no *to a solicitor on the phone. Each one is practice.*

We might begin to like no's *more than we ever thought we would. Our* no's *might become gentler and yet more penetrating and truthful. They might enter the hidden pockets of avoidance and cowardice that each of us has. Our lives would come cleaner and our love more visible even if we must disappoint someone we love.*

When we say no *to someone they are allowed to see where we stand.*

Saying *Yes*

How easy it is to say yes when the heart is open and connected! It's as easy as breathing. Fundamentally we want to say yes to life, to love and to committed work. The trouble is that we are prone to say too many yeses. Just as a considered no clears the way for a considered yes, so a considered yes implies many no's for life to come into order and integrity.

This is as demanding in a close friendship as it is elsewhere in life, though it tends to get muddier there since we feel a deep draw towards our friends. Isn't it better, for instance, to see each other a little less, if when we are face to face our yes is imbued with a quality of full presence? Another example might be that we take the time to discern where we can help the other the most and let smaller giving impulses go unattended.

To receive is a yes and takes vital energy also. When we are habitual givers we forget what that might mean to the one who is to receive what we habitually give. If what is given is on the mark, we receive easily and openly. In other circumstances, let's admit that receiving can be work and we must be able to say no thank you.

With yes and no our way unfolds. Unless we are aware we simply react instead of mindfully act. Within the opportunity of a conscious friendship this could be a wonderful area to explore. We would learn how profound is a no or a yes. They are the breath of giving and receiving.

ଊଊ

On a day we must make a choice, could we place our no in the left, more subordinate hand, and our yes in our right, more dominant hand? The left hand and arm are closer to the heart. The right hand is closer to our habits of being. For left-handed people this may be experienced differently.

Might we, with this little game, grant our body's heart side the task of saying no and our right more discriminating side the task of being open-handed and saying yes?

The usual circuits are switched. Our bodies might sense something differently than what our minds know. Putting our hands together, not only will there be a different sensation but a different quality of experience. Our choices will be full bodied.

Daily we discriminate with yes and no. In our special friendships could we help one another to be not only faithful but even handed?

Conflict

Even in the deepest and most chosen relationships, conflicts arise. Our points of view collide in some unsolvable way. *Yes* finds only *No* and vice versa. We feel distraught with the very person we would be constant with. The tendency when things are so is to try to *solve* the rupture instead of embracing it. Giving in to each other is not what deep friends should make practice of.

Real differences of opinion that lead us to choices away from each other become those opportunities to increase what love and commitment are all about. When we draw a circle and declare that within its precinct we can be in accord, we limit our world. How freeing it is when we make that circle either bigger or something entirely else--a space where opposite points of view can still be in relationship.

To agree to disagree can lead us to new ideas of what is possible. The open hand of love lets go and remains open. In conflict we learn to allow some primal fears just to be: fear that we will lose our friendship and so be abandoned--fear that we will be asked to live something we cannot or will not live--fear that we are not able to perform what the other needs or wants—fear that our resources will not be sufficient—and many more.

Simply put, we must give fear time and space and kindness. To be faithful in the midst of misunderstanding is more a proof of love than any quick patch-up that lets us out of a sticky place.

ಬಬ

Misunderstandings are not as specific as we make them out to be. They carry moods and usually a past that has nothing to do with the present. We may need to look for where and when we had similar troubles in our history—troubles we have brought unknowingly to the present.

We can realize that this is true for our friend as well. We must rely on patience and kindness to give us time for understanding. Emotional space, mutually given, is an enormous gift. We can understand that something larger than is apparent is happening to us both.

When our friend gives us time and does not shut the door on us, we can feel how we are still joined beyond what is happening. We sense how much larger we are than our fears.

Prayer

An obvious aspect of faithfulness between deep friends is that we pray for each other. When we have a need of some kind, we hear people say, I hold you in the Light, or I hold you in heart and mind. We are glad of that, of course. But what about holding each other in prayer for no specific reason at all and for the best reason--to be faithful? Do we allow ourselves to experience that we are carried in one another's intercession?

Mostly we note it mentally as a nice thing, but we often don't take the time to incorporate the fact--take it into our body. Could we not only pray for each other daily but also take the time to receive those prayers? Prayer is substantial and has both weight and direction. It has heat, strength and duration. In prayer we are given more than we can ever digest or understand.

Prayer, for and with each other, is a profound conviction that Love is taking place and that we, in our smallness, are tapping into the very immensity that created the universe. Sacred writings amply testify that we can experience this.

Beyond conflict and tension, beyond the yes's and

no's of our lives, when we place our heart's friend in the radiant mystery of God's love and remain with them there in trust, we do one of the most faithful things we can do as companions on the way.

∽∾

When we pray for our friend we are also incorporated into the prayer because prayer is a dynamic give and take. We are mutually infused and re-created in profound and subtle ways that can be verified as our lives unfold. .

Sometimes we will feel the sending of prayer more—at other times the receiving. But in the end, sending and receiving tend to merge. There is no sender and no receiver. There is just prayer happening.

We could decide ahead of time to be at prayer at a specific time and feel that we are together though we may actually be miles apart. We know how electricity runs a computer as well as a toaster. Love like a current of electricity flows into our friendship when we connect to it, and then we are given energy in ways we each need and so much more besides.

Compassion

It is easy for us to pity others. It doesn't cost us much. When we pity we are safely away from any real, gut level participation in suffering. Compassion, on the other hand, asks us to respond from our viscera. To be in each other's lives with compassion means that we are in a profound participatory comprehension.

It is about being truly human together. We extend the balm of empathy to one another instead of feeling sorry for each other. We learn to be balanced and useful in the midst of difficulty. We offer the stability of companionship when it is needed, and together our lives take part in the larger context of community. So intimate is compassion that it brings the world and its wounds into our very breath. We know that each of us is because we all are.

Balm

Compassion is that stirring of the heart that lets us participate with others in the trials of life. Without it we would be in a very cold world. Sorrows that are shared are more bearable. Carried with another they become means of transformation and transcendence. In them and through them we bond.

Compassion invites us to know we are not isolated, not forgotten or alone. Whether we are in the giving or the receiving end of it, the very fact that another knows where we are is like coming out of darkness. Compassion is not only seeing the truth with our minds, but it is also feeling it fully. This is participatory knowing. We are brought out of isolation when someone feels with us but does not identify with us.

This is hard to explain. To feel another's difficulty of whatever nature without becoming enmeshed with them is a great act of awareness. On the receiving end of this equation we can sense that we are lovingly witnessed rather than emotionally entangled. Then our own tears become significant and real to us. We taste the salt in them. We feel their wet presence on our faces. We *realize* them as ours.

Together we know that in the depths of pain Spirit is at work. With each other's compassion we can be more vulnerable and undefended. It is a great balm. The path is not around, but through what life brings. With each other's empathy we are able to live what we must and dare to feel all of it.

∽∾

In the dictionary the definition for empathy is: "an imaginative projection of one's own consciousness into another's being." We can only imagine the suffering that our friends are undergoing, and so our responses cannot be as mirrors that reflect just what is in front of us. Our responses to suffering will be colored and shaped by our own experience.

Though we will never fully feel or exactly understand the suffering of a friend, we are more alike as human beings than we are different. We can hope and trust that the mutuality our friends feel from us covers the mistakes we might make in responding to their pain.

Pity

Compassion is not pity yet it often masks that emotion. Pity has distance in it. We set ourselves away from what we pity. We are perhaps even secretly disapproving of that which is being pitied. We can also be afraid of it, so we cover our fear with a mask of pity. We are then feeling "for" another with secret superiority or with relief that we have escaped the fate we are observing. These are but two examples of how we might be distancing from someone we feel we ought to have empathy for.

This is subtle and degrading to both parties. When we pity we are often simply avoiding pain and will give money, advice and personal efforts to not feel what we imagine the other to be feeling. In compassion we behave quite differently. It isn't that we are trying to feel what the other person feels or to rescue them from their fate. It is that we are willing to be present with the ones we love in their pain and with our own discomforts about their pain without masking anything.

Often we don't have such maturity. But when we are able to do this even a little, it is experienced as a gift. We sense that our heart's friend has not dismissed us in do-goodness, in subtle judgment, or in rescue operations of one kind or another. We sense they are there *with* us—love with love, fear with fear—helplessness with helplessness—joined in the vulnerability and mystery of being human. In that sense of solidarity the heart cracks wide open and lets Spirit in.

∽

Relieving suffering where we can is natural, yet we are not to mask pain or take it away because we learn so much in it and through it. In compassion, our friend's pain, and the suffering we feel witnessing that pain, merges as one. We can't do compassion. We can only be it.

Could we be near one another when we suffer and allow each other to experience what we must without avoidance? When we do that, we give to each other in an immense way. Together we are able to be in the hells that sometime happen in life and still feel we have light.

Balance

To sustain compassion is difficult when there are chronic conditions such as ill health or sustained losses. Such continuous experiences are hard on both parties, and learning to have compassion for our selves in such situations is a necessity.

In the face of pain, feeling sorry for our selves, or the opposite--ignoring our selves or suppressing our selves--are all efforts at management. We know management isn't compassion. It is control and efficiency. Could we imagine a see saw--one end will go up if there is enough weight to make the opposite side go down? Feeling anger, pity or resentment will tip the balance. The heavy side goes down and throws much up in the air. Ignoring our own feelings and needs is a dead weight also though we might not know it. Down goes the seesaw and up goes disconnection and distraction.

A loved friend's loss or difficulty will make an impact on us, and because it does, it is even more incumbent on us to find the inner balance that lets us live in and with things as they are. When we neither ignore what is happening or feel victimized by it, we find a middle ground where the big swings of feeling can be balanced. A lived compassion actually has an objective center to it. It helps us be with pain without identifying with it. Able to witness pain, feel it and not merge with it, we are spacious and have left reactivity behind for Love's sake.

∾

Anxiety and fear vibrate in our bodies. They are fast emotions that stir up our nervous systems. We feel antsy and scattered. These emotions send urgent signals to find immediate solutions.

It is here that we need compassion. When everything cries out for action, we can sit in the center of it all, allowing thought and emotion to come to balance and so enable us to turn from reactivity and management to real feeling, that rooted place on that level place on the see saw where we can dangle our legs into uncertainty and still relax.

Not trapped by reactivity we know that solutions are hidden within our problems. We also understand that sometimes there are no solutions--things will not change for the better. We must accept them as they are.

Companionship

As companions we remind each other that we are always living within the context of a vast Love that suffers in us and through us. We exist in a continuous Compassion. As we turn our suffering over to that Companionship, something profound happens to us.

Often the circumstances have not changed nor have our own discomforts, but we can sense an inner strength, a knowledge that nothing of our experience is skipped over or dismissed as valueless. Our suffering has both purpose and meaning.

No longer will we identify ourselves as victims nor gloss over the difficulties we find ourselves in. It is in conscious suffering that Love is present. Together in that Mystery we feel our vulnerability transformed into something luminous.

This can be practiced when small afflictions befall us. Feeling a *poor me* coming on, we remind each other to invite the loving presence of Spirit and to remember we are not alone. Shared suffering is shared truth and opens us to more acceptance. Practicing this way does not mean we are anticipating terrible things. On the contrary, we are learning to be inwardly free. In small, daily ways we grow the habit of being free no matter what.

ᘍᘓ

When we are inconvenienced or made uncomfortable for any reason, could we interrupt our automatic responses to feel singled out by misfortune? Most likely we won't be able to do this easily, but as deep friends we can help each other. The mind has such good arguments to keep us in old juicy patterns of victimization. But we always have the option to lean into Spirit. There we learn to see beyond our little context to a greater sense of things.

Forgetful and entrenched in habits as we are, we can be nudged back into living from the core and the cure—Spirit holding us with constant companionship.

Community

As loving friends we are mirrors of compassion for each other, reflecting the joy and ache of being the ones we have been given to be. And we can also be those self same mirrors reflecting compassion for our immediate worlds of family and community. Most of us cannot range much further.

We know from science, however, that we exist in a unified field. Since this is so, what is done in love and awareness, though it may be small and local, has impact on the whole. We can practice close to home with that understanding, offering that which is ours to do while knowing that it spreads in mysterious ways beyond our small circumstances.

Together with a heart's friend it is easier to respond to community needs and to bring our compassion into concrete action. The need for inclusion, understanding, remembrance and support is continuous.

Compassion can be so powerful for some people that they are willing to risk their lives. Perhaps we can risk more time, more of our financial resources, more of our skills because we are inwardly moved. To reflect one another's passion for the aches in the world is central in a serious friendship. We see how we each love—how we each *must* love.

If we are not drawn to the same endeavors, we can nevertheless know the feeling of the heart's pull and that nothing of love is ever lost. Once given, it continues though we may never know exactly how.

ΩΩ

If challenge, work, suffering and joy are the bricks, then compassion is the mortar that holds things together and creates structures we can live in. That mortar must be mixed every day to be usable. It must be applied without pity or carelessness but with loving attention. Compassion is a balm. It teaches balance. It gives us companionship and community.

As we experience it, we become more ourselves. Real empathy has no strategy to it, no sense of personal gain It simply is. Mixed with the living water from our hearts it can be liberally used wherever it is needed to hold what must be held.

In compassion we are the givers, the receivers and the gift all at once. It takes place simultaneously everywhere. Even now we are receivers of compassion given by others from distant places and other times.

Respect

How many marriages, partnerships, and friendships founder because there is a basic lack of respect between the partners? All respect that is conditional—that is given because someone is attractive, smart, helpful, earns a great salary, has wonderful connections, dresses well, is wealthy,etc.—is respect that in the final analysis is based on function rather than on essence. These qualities are nice, of course, and we are often initially drawn to a person because of them. But these functions can start to feel old and be less and less important. We long to be respected for the one we essentially are, not for what we can provide.

Respect has to do with character, with presence and trustworthiness. It is our service to life itself that shines through even when our limitations are obvious. When we come to know that our essential value is not in questions we then receive our being as a gift beyond price, and we understand that it will take our whole lifetime to return that gift. How can respect be absent from this?

Consideration

We know respect isn't dumb awe of another. Respect is a dynamic, mutual condition in which both persons can experience themselves as worthy of deep consideration. There are so many ways to respect another person. Could we notice the people we pass in the street, the people who help us with ordinary tasks--the clerk at the bank, the man who delivers fuel to the house, the waitress, the dental assistant . . . on and on?

A first respectful act is to be aware of these persons--to see them *in themselves*. The second act would be to recognize that they belong, as we do, in the family of man. In a very short time ordinary transactions would carry an unspoken quality of courtesy.

Living this way, we would take out of our engagements the tendency to treat each other as functions rather than as persons. Any time we do that we've lost respect for ourselves without knowing it. We become efficient rather than human. We demand and expect instead of request and receive. Our demanding makes us exploitative when the very same transactions we have many times a day could be between two equal humans.

What about this in our friendships? How often do we have hidden expectations of ourselves and of each other? These expectations carry silent demands. This is slippery territory. We harm our true connection in mazes of disregard and assumptions when we forget that every person is far more than the roles they fulfill. We are of infinite value.

༓

Though we fall into unconscious disregard now and then, who would be better to learn with than our friend who already appreciates our value? Simply that we are is of benefit and beauty. The very least measure of respect we give to one another is to know this.

When film is developed the image forms on the paper little by little in the developing fluid until it is there in bright detail. Mutual respect is like developing fluid. Little by little we see each other more vividly and realize how holy and fragile our particularity is. We are unique and sacred truths, and we are here such a very short time.

Service

nother part of mutual respect is to confirm that Life is working on itself in each of us. We may be privileged by a close friendship to have glimpses of what that may be, but we will never fully penetrate the mystery of it. We are each an alchemical vessel where meaning is taking place. We are formed and reformed by life, and Spirit is at work within us.

We are not only the place where Spirit is at work, but we are also that which is being worked. Therefore we cannot *from the outside* presume to know what ultimately is being formed. We can only watch, wait and wonder as the mystery takes place in us and between us.

Just as we would not, except in deep ignorance, invade and take over a service of worship we might be attending, so also, if we understand a human life to be a service of worship, we would not enter another's sacred ritual with our own notions of *what should take place.*

Spirit asks us to be particular and distinct, but being unique is not a license to have our way, or to not be in co-operation. On the contrary, it is only as unique beings that a vital relationship becomes possible. We absolutely need the *otherness* of the other.

So it is that when we watch, wait and wonder with the friend of our heart we are in a kind of holy service. We can sense that we are actually waiting upon Spirit in each other, and that makes us truer servants of life.

෴

Respect could be thought of as a dance where steps are taken together and separately to music that grants the dancers freedom. We cannot dance with someone who steps on our toes or holds us so tightly that we cannot breathe.

A dance can have contrapuntal aspects. It can be fast for one and slow for another at the same time and still be in rhythm. What lets us dance well together is taking each other into account.

On an actual dance floor we notice where others might be headed. We do not hoard the floor. We can train ourselves to remember that relationships share an emotional dance floor.

When we take care of the relationship first, many ways to dance are possible. This is a flow we know to be respect made visible.

Trust

When we stand outside of our deep friendships for a moment and look in on the dancers, we would surely see the gestures, steps and patterns of each of us and how they coincide. We would see the whole gestalt between the dancers. Watching we would recognize that the dancers have given themselves to their inner music and to the dance as well as to each other. If as deep friends we give ourselves to spiritual consciousness there is a commitment present that is beyond the personal which then holds both our individual and our mutual movements in life.

There will be many times when we do not understand something one of us says or does. Yet when we respect that we are committed to Spirit we can allow much though it may appear strange to us. We listen for the sacred tune in the other. We trust that Spirit is making music in each of us. We learn to trust that fact as much as we trust one another.

Many things come into our lives that we do not want to dance with, yet often those discordant melodies are part of completeness. We are not to live without challenges—rather we are to dance *with* them—not *to* them.

When we respect that our friends have given themselves to their inner music as we have done, we can better hold any difficulties, confusions or misunderstandings we might have. We continue dancing together through both suffering and bliss.

ಬಜ

How wordless is music! We are drawn by it into reveries and moods of all kinds. Our friendships, too, are held in a kind of vibration, a frequency of comfort and familiarity. It's not hard to sense a vibe in a moment in time or in the atmosphere of a room. We call them good vibes or bad vibes. We don't have to explain what we mean. We simply feel them.

There are spiritual frequencies, too, that require that we sense beyond what we know and can name, beyond our likes and dislikes, our habits and preferences. Spirit asks us to be connected beyond differences. There are no explanations, no analysis, nor any particular way that can be spelled out for the way Spirit vibrates within us. We must simply respect that this interior frequency is and let the connections beyond understanding move us into more and more meaningful ways to dance with life.

Limitation

An area more difficult perhaps than others, but nevertheless vital, is to respect our own and our beloved's limitations. We can grow. We can change. We can mature and we can deepen. A classical and difficult way to do this is to respect our limits.

In a bowl, for instance, it is within its limits that something can be held. When we can go from respecting our limits to being able to care for them, a profound change takes place. Right there, on the edge of what we are and can do at any given time, we encounter the necessity of limits. Whole worlds exist precisely at such junctures.

Respecting our limits we become liminal--dwellers in that space where the known and the unknown meet, where the darkness of life and the light of life intermingle, where Spirit moves us because we have softened enough to accept our limitations and yet opened enough to not be defined by them. Just there, in that paradox, we are surely met by love.

When we do not fight with the limitations of our beloved friends (perceived from our point of view, of course) and they do not fight with our limitations (perceived from their point of view), we have grace and space. When we do not fight with ourselves either, because of where we are and what we can and cannot do, we enter into the depths of transformation. Trust is made visible and humility is born--that quiet agent of possibility and hard won peace.

ॐ

Day after day as we age we will know limitations of all kinds. Day after day these limits can help us grow in spiritual ways. Perhaps we become more loving, more patient, more tolerant of differences, more sure of what we want to give and more able to discern what no longer belongs.

We help each other see the best uses of our present abilities. We help each other sense the small, doable ways we are able to give of ourselves even as we diminish. A limitation is always and end and a beginning at the same time. It is a profound place of growth.

Without our limitations we would not be our selves. All of us long to be loved as we are with our limits. And isn't that the limitless way that Spirit loves us even now?

Presence

To be deeply respectful of another we must first be respectful of ourselves. We are all unfinished works in progress. There is always a place we can improve. But becoming excellent, good or fault free is not the goal, though we might have erroneously been taught that in our youth.

Not defined by our goals, we can actually become more self-respecting. Think of how many ways our egos are negotiating for a place to be acceptable. If only we could lose those ten pounds... If we could only get that job, or have that relationship... If only we were embraced by that group of powerful people...etc. etc. etc. All that striving is striving for our own conditional respect. It's important to know that self-respect and self-love are different. It is possible to have the one without the other.

Our goals are not the culprit. We need them to get anything done, but when we use them as the currency of self-respect we are using them in the wrong way. Could we instead become more present? Could we meet our joy, our despair, our confusion, our anger and our silliness without disapproval or approval? Could we show up and not dismiss or disparage ourselves or make more of ourselves than we are.

Being present to just what is true is the most respectful we can be. We can safely go to the limit on that one! Able to show up as we actually are for our inner life's sake, would we not be more able to be present to one dear to our heart?

တတ

We do not learn best by fear, by avoidance or by pleasing, but by trial and error, by discovery and surprise. We learn by going where we need to go.

Mutual respect requires consideration, trust and presence. It reaches us less in applause and approval than by the acceptance of our limitations and differences — the whole and unvarnished truth about us. That is respect we can believe in.

In owning our beauty and our less than best, we are given a chance to experience that we are already held in love and that even our limps are put to use in good ways.

Self-Approval

Self-approval and self-acceptance are very different. In self-approval we get check marks for the good we think we do, for the fine impressions we think we make. There is a kind of tallying of merit that happens—so many good marks and we can earn our own conditional approval.

But in self-acceptance there is no tally sheet. There are no check marks. There is, instead, an inner transparency. We own how we project on others what we have not yet worked through. We are aware of how we resist knowing the ways we hide so we can be what we call *safe*.

We confess both our beauty and our faults and are open to forgiveness. Worthiness then comes to us as a matter of course. We do not earn it. It is a given we can humbly accept as fundamental and true.

Projection

I t's hard to respect and love another fully until we respect and love ourselves. This is an obvious truth, but hard to live. As much as we may want to love our heart's friend with complete freedom and depth, we may not be able to. Aspects of ourselves that we have not yet learned to know and love into healing and maturity get in the way.

It is usually in the deep loves of our lives that pockets of unworthiness surface. The very safety of love seems to give permission for that which is unloved to emerge. When we are safe, open and vulnerable, we are also easily re-injured.

As loving friends we try to see each other as well as we can, but we are destined to be faulty witnesses from time to time. The parts we enjoy, admire and are happy about are what attract us to each other. We sense an affinity with what we see either because we have it as a capacity as well, or we have it as a potential to be developed. When we find ourselves in criticism, disappointment, anger and confusion we have run into a negative projection of some kind. No matter how we were provoked, we have nevertheless found a pocket of unworthiness that belongs to us to work on.

Side by side we can witness and be part of a rich process of growing. Ultimately we are the ones responsible for ourselves. Coming into wholeness is our soul's task and ours alone.

ແ໙ຉ

Whatever can develop in our soul is ours to cultivate, but it is not ours to determine. We will each always be in process—called into deeper truthfulness and humility.

We live in a mystery—one that we cannot fully understand. We each carry an abyss of separateness that makes us alone. It is a particularity that, in which and through which, we can come to wholeness and to God.

As deep friends we see each other off into the inner wilderness. The necessity for alone time is real, and it becomes blessed into solitude by Spirit—not by our actions or our talking. In that silence—alone with aloneness—another reality takes over. As projection shrinks we can perceive one another as belonging to God.

Resistance

Learning self-acceptance is one insult after the other. In contrast, self-knowledge is easier for it is information about our selves. But information is not acceptance. We all have inner-reservations-- many we are unaware of. These reservations shape our stance in life. To surrender to the truth of them when there is no one to hold us is chilling.

We resist in so many ways. We judge, demand, argue, control and insist that we, and others, should be different than they are or than we are. We often do this subtly, but we are doing it nevertheless. Listening to any ordinary conversation reveals how often we think we know best. We may also space out, occupying ourselves in countless ways, many of them even useful. We are resisting by default, distracted by things that are not fundamental to us. Or we lose ourselves in illusions, making ourselves seem important and entitled, or making others out to be so.

We cling to things as well; things we believe will do it for us. We grasp after acknowledgement, persons, circumstances and things we think will enhance us. Ultimately no outward thing will do it for us.

It is in solitude that we come to know the countless ways we resist. Alone we have a chance to hold hands with our avoidance and face the truth that we are essentially powerless. Befriending powerlessness is a royal road. The sovereignty found there will not be taken from us.

∞

Alone in a wild place in nature most of us feel small.

The empty sky appears enormous, the dark night endless, the forest impenetrable. Inner places can feel the same to us. Our imaginations exaggerate the difficulties we have to face and our thoughts drag us into all kinds of wilderness.

These are the dark nights. We are trapped in the jungle of confusion, alone in an arid desert of anger or a swamp of grief. We want to run away from experiencing any of it, or we want to fight with it to some bitter end.

A deeper truth is there also—that we are, and have been, fundamentally naked and powerless all along, yet we belong to the whole to God's huge inclusiveness. And we are worthy of care.

Confession

In time we find that all the ways of avoiding our inner truth do not work. We sense that we are living in the scaffolding of resistance and insistence, not in the solid home of self-acceptance. Scaffolding is important when we are repairing a building, but it is in the way when we want to live in it.

Acceptance is not approval. It is bigger than that. Approval gives a positive focus, but a focus nevertheless. It pin points. Acceptance gives us space as wide as the sky and renders approval unimportant.

Neither is acceptance agreement. Though pleasing, agreement is also limiting. Acceptance appears meek and docile but it is the opposite. It is dynamic and inclusive. It offers room without capitulation. It is, in fact, confession.

We cannot have acceptance without confession. When our faults are truly confessed we have accepted their existence. Curiously it is then they seem to shrink and they come into a new proportion. Less judged and resisted they change and diminish of their own accord. We find that in essence they were thwarted desires that needed to be filled in better ways.

Confessed, our beauty and goodness changes. It grows, and with more room we may find we have talents for things we were not aware of. We may also dare new things. Without judgment we expand and experiment. Living in self-acceptance we live in an ongoing confession, a home with many doors and windows that invites the world to live *with* us.

ഌ

When we first move into the home of self-acceptance it is usually a little place—something small to inhabit and feel cozy in now and then. As we acknowledge more of the truth about ourselves we learn that this inner home has doors with no locks, that there are unknown rooms within it for us to make our own.

Acceptance grows in the light of confession and experience. Room upon room continues to open. There are always new dimensions to find and to live in. Slowly we understand that this home, which we believed to be small, is really a mansion of spaciousness, Nothing is left out. There is room for all that we are and can be. Acceptance is the longed for home of the heart.

Forgiveness

I t is not enough to know that we said or did something that hurt us, or another. The acceptance of
the facts is essential. So is the acceptance of our
regrets and our self-judgments about what happened.
These are the preambles of forgiveness. Even though
we understand *all of that*, to experience that we are forgiven is a deeper matter.

We can't *do* forgiveness. It is something that is *done
in* and *for* us. To forgive and to be forgiven is a mystery
we open to. We cannot force it or manufacture it in any
way. To experience remorse is a needed step. It is a beginning. To continue to be remorseful over and over is
actually inverted pride. We are the judge, the jury and
the convict. Being right about how wrong we are, aren't
we still playing God?

If we are to give or to receive forgiveness, we must
turn towards the source of forgiveness. It is in the mystery of God's love that our self-betrayals and failures
find rest. It is in Love's deep embrace that we wait. It
is a profound silence where our shame can be transformed.

We will never be fully conscious of what transpires

in that unfathomable stillness. But we can trust ourselves to it. We can attend it with our whole being and lean into it. In time we may see signs of release. Old pain leaves the cells of our bodies and dissolves. We feel lighter. Muted like an old photograph the past grows soft around the edges. It is another dawn in which we see light around old issues and the glimmer of new beginnings.

ख़

We sit by the door of silence with our old familiars—shame and remorse. Though we still do many things out in the world, we are also inwardly sitting in front of that closed door for days, months and years. We are waiting upon love.

We don't know if the door will ever open. Yet if we persist and sit with longing, we can feel that under our failures is a yearning that calls to the Love behind the silence.

On the day the door opens, as if on its own, we step out and over the threshold. We are met by the Presence that fills us and leads us and has waited with us on both sides of the door.

Worthiness

Our worthiness is there from the beginning. We have simply forgotten that we entered life "trailing clouds of glory", and that when we depart all we have learned of love will be our passport.

Worthiness is a wondrous thing. It is softer than skin and holds the knowledge that all is gift--our lives, our opportunities and even our suffering. Worthiness was given to us with our first breath. We need only to draw another breath to recall that we are inspired ones. Breath by breath we are to give away everything we have received. This is not poverty. It is the wealth of self-expression.

In sharing our gifts they multiply, and we become ourselves more and more. However small our offerings may seem to us, there are countless ways these gifts are received. We will not know the full extent of this. Does a tree know who or what benefits from the oxygen it produces? It must give to be alive. We, too, must give to be alive.

When we wear our worthiness the way leaves clothe a tree or the stars bespangle the sky, we are clothed in a mantle of grace. We own the preciousness of our lives

and know them to be treasures, ones we have a lifetime
to share.

ೞೞ

*A new life begins when we consciously wake to the holy
worth of our being. We wash our faces with the air of
morning. Having confessed our projections, our resistance
and our need for forgiveness, we can take up the work of
our hands with a sense of wonder—that we are continually
forgiven and have a part to play and ways to serve the larger
purpose.*

*Day after day we spend ourselves. Even when we are
old and can only smile and breathe, our worth extends into
hidden places beyond our knowing. Our worth is not ours.
It belongs to Life. We are its treasures.*

Longing

There is always longing going on within us. We are born with desires: first for food, safety and emotional connection. As infants we reach into life with those drives. As vulnerable as we are, the desire to live and have our needs met is a fierce one that far outweighs our size.

Later in life our deep longings are often felt in a more diffuse way. They may even be obscure or dulled. We have vague sensations that hint that we have more possibilities than we are living. These hints are nudges from *the beyond within*. The unknown beckons. We feel a fearful kind of excitement.

Since we cannot go where we have not imaged, we need dreams. Without dreams our souls shrivel. We need images of what might be possible for us, icons that inspire us onward. We need our deep friend to believe that we can achieve the longings of our heart. We need to believe that Spirit wants our passion to be made visible for our own sake and for the sake of all that is.

Possibilities

B y embracing our worth we touch our deep longings also. On a spiritual level we know we are
called to be something for all of existence, however humble it might be. This calling is like a vital seed.
It waits inside sometimes for decades, and it needs our
engagement in order to be lived.

Hints about this calling comes to us throughout life
though we often ignore them. We do not realize that
these tiny signals point to something larger—a possibility that is unique to us and ours to develop. Our friends
can help us to notice these hints and to act on them.
There is an impulse logic to them. We must not think
of these nudges as irrelevant nonsense, impulsivity or
ego gratification. These nudges that lie deep within are
dynamic. They ask us to feel, to engage and to commit
to action on behalf of our essence. They never have *profit*
or *self-enhancement* as a primary objective. They are simply
asking for circumstances that will let them grow and be
expressed. A heart's friend can give us support to find
and engage our longings.

It is from these levels that people will give their
lives for another, spend years in causes they believe in,

enter into experiences very different from what they have previously known. It is from these depths that we can create beauty and meaning where there was none before. When our seed longings are nudged and given encouragement from a true friend we can feel how everything inside wants to say *yes*.

ର

We may in quiet, in conversation or even in passing, sense that something is awake within us. We may feel it when we hear a certain kind of music. A painting may sweep us into its beauty. The smooth working of a machine may ignite invention within us. A thorny problem lures us into puzzling and scientific investigation. We are filled with vitality when we are triggered

Hints come unexpectedly and often in un-dramatic ways. They nudge an inner capacity that is unique to us and ours to develop. As loving friends we can be aware that soul seeds lie fallow and dormant within us. Together we can challenge and help each other dare find ways to live them.

Fears

When we were young we may have played *dare you* to gain the courage to do something we were afraid to do. *Dare you to jump in the water. Dare you to climb over the fence. Dare you to open the cellar door and go down in the dark.* We were dealing with childhood fears. As adults we still deal with fear. To dare to act on our deep desires can still feel like jumping into deep water without knowing where bottom is.

As adults our fears are less about physical safety. We fear looking stupid. We fear failing at what we try, or finding that what we desired isn't what it's cracked up to be. We fear we've no talent for things we long for.

Fear is loud and has many voices. It keeps saying *what if* and lists all the negative outcomes we could imagine. But with a true friend we can listen to another voice saying *what if*--a voice that imagines possibility.

For instance, a friend who know us to have an artistic longing might say: *What if you took an art class? What if you doodled every day for the sheer fun of it? What if you made your own greeting cards? What if you are not a professional artist but have fun trying? What if loving color and form you make beauty every day as you build or garden or set the table or arrange your tools? What if beauty is what you are and these small but significant are ways that you can recognize this truth.*

In whatever area that draws us, playing *what if* will nurture our seed longings, helping them to shed their shells, to open and to take root.

৯৫৯

Over time we come to know where we limp and where we soar, and what unnecessary cages we live in from which we long to be free.

When we intuit for each other we are playing what if. *Imagined possibilities and suggestions fly between us. They are playful ideas that do not demand an outcome. We are simply asking each other to think in winged ways.*

When one of those insights resonates with us, we can begin to feather out into possibility. Significant inspirations always bring us energy and hope. They may even allow us to let go of fear and try our wings.

Dreams

When we buy vegetable or flower seeds we get them in packets with pictures and planting instructions. We know what to expect when the seeds germinate. Soul seeds don't come with instructions or guaranteed outcomes. Following our deep desires we live by trial and error, not by trial and perfect. Errors are part of our journey. Embraced they have a chance to be changed into blessings.

Because we don't know what kind of seeds we have inside, we must cultivate them in order to recognize them. Even with insight we don't get a sense of the whole or of how seemingly disparate things might be brought together. Here our heart's friend is so very helpful. When we are afraid we encourage each other to remember that uncertainty is the birthplace of courage. We remind each other that where certainty is a closed book, uncertainty allows for possibility. We hold one another's errors lightly, knowing they are detours that will eventually take us around to where we can continue our journey.

When we help each other dream it is like gardening. We water, feed, and protect one another from wind and harsh rain. We look for each other's growth and re-member that germination times can be slow and that all the right circumstances of weather and nutrients must be there for things to emerge. We know all work in manifestation is the work of human love joined to the Great Love that always creates with us.

తించి

Dreaming forward—what is it but the careful use of all senses plus a sixth? It is a kind of Braille. We are feeling our way—sensing and pausing—not hurrying—intimately touching the next possibility with thought and care.

When we go at that loving pace we are less likely to dream wrongly. We will be informed—one hand tracing the page of life—the other giving support. Our core already knows something our lives must discover. But could it also be that we are being discovered? Even as we think we are doing the dreaming, could it be that we are being dreamed? Could we be open to that thought? Could we become what Life wants us to be?

Images

We need representations of our dreams, to feel them, sense them, and clothe them with outward visible signs of our inward longing. Desires that are deeply pictured and bodily felt are prayers in and of themselves. Aristotle said that, "the soul never thinks without an image." Picturing our deep longings with a special friend is a doubled prayer. To picture is not only visual. Some people hear their images, feel them as sensation, or experience them in other ways. However it happens, our deep desires move into being when we become aware of the images that represent them. Like icons they have power and work inside us in mysterious ways.

The longing for inner freedom, for instance, is a bodily sensation, an emotional reality and a way of living in the world. A photo of a dancer in the ecstasy of dance might be an icon for such a longing. Looked at daily it is a motivation as well as a visual prayer. The desire to be more centered might be a beautiful calligraphy of a circle or a wide branching tree. To be of service might be pictured of as a pair of open hands. We help each other by looking for those images that evoke our longing. Strangely, once our longings are felt more, it seems that appropriate images cross our path as if by magic. Spirit enters the unconscious through the use of these guiding pictures and awaken their possibility in us. Using them we develop a stronger and stronger disposition towards our hearts' desires and for ways to live them.

༺༻

We would not have found a soul-guiding image unless we were ready for it. The seeds of our longing wait, as all seeds do, for the right time and the right conditions. With our heart's friend we can better trust ourselves to waiting and to trust itself.

When we wait upon something we serve it and antici- pate it. It is a deeply creative process. When we have waited on an image long enough it becomes integrated. We no lon- ger need it because the sparkle it held for us is now inside. We are ready for another image to show us where to grow. There is no end to this growing as long as we are alive.

Fruition

We desire many outward things that we believe will make our lives richer and more joyous. They may be jobs, partners, homes, fame, fun, wealth, adventure, etc. Underneath these desires are the deeper longings: yearning for time, for soulful relatedness, for peace, for simplicity, for meaningful service, for self-expression and beauty. These longings can be sensed as Life longing for us to be its lovers. We are to fulfill that mandate abundantly--to have life and to be life. Could we trust that Spirit is always working with us to bring our deep desires into being, to bring us to wholeness?

Sometimes that wholeness can only come to us through suffering. Suffering re-directs us from paths that do not lead to the deepest longings we have. Illness may bring with it the time we have yearned for. Lost love may bring us into greater self-love. Peace may come to us when we give up false effort around things that can never bring us peace. Loss of work may lead us into paths that have service as their essence. Suffering we may learn to value small, significant things we never valued before. Something we can be sure of is that love is at work in the depth of our longing. This yearning never ends. It is a red thread imbedded in our lives, an artery. To stop yearning is to be bloodless. We cannot be without longing. As heart friends we know that what we deeply long for is what Spirit also longs for within us.

໑໑

Serving the deep longings of our being we hold each other to the central task of our lives—to embody our core. Despite the fears we might have we look for possibilities and guiding images. We dream each other forward and do not skip over the small, radiant chances to love, to notice and to help.

When we create something new, we are aware that we are that place of potency where Love is working on itself to bring about fruition. Serving our soul's longing we know it to be praise.

Loving

To love and be loved is a longing all of us have. The way love reaches us is different for each of us, and how deeply we allow it to enter us is a lifetime's work.

We are nourished and shaped by human love or lack of it,but we are rendered whole by the love Spirit has for us. It is there that all we are and all we can become are held in infinite tenderness and compassion. How we arrive at knowing this and feeling it as true for us is a central task of deep friendship.

It is within a human framework of compassion and respect that we can begin to sense and eventually experience how Spirit yearns for us and for our wholeness. We give each loving awareness and it leads us in time to the Presence, to Spirit, our deepest friend.

Confidence

In a deep friendship we have those fertilizing moments when something is mutually confirmed. This recognition is a place of germination--a place brought to life by the presence of the other. We keep alive the truest parts of each other--that edge of growth where both excitement and necessity come together. At that convergence there is a dynamic energy that does not want to be denied.

How do we love this way? We know by now that we do so first by Recognition, but we also do so by a visceral trust that the other will be true to his or her edge of possibility. It is a gut faith in each other's courage and tempo. Where we might experience urgency or reluctance, our friend will remind us that Spirit is at work in us and that growth happens in many curious ways--sometimes allowing periods of rest, or periods in which we suffer adversity, or even periods of wallowing in discouragement.

Visceral trust is not a thought. It's not prayer but a certitude--a lighted window in the dark. We stay awake on each other's behalf even if one of us is plodding through the most tangled of undergrowths in a wood too far away for any light to be seen.

We are not rescued by our heart's friend so much as *awaited* in trust and confidence.

ॐ

To be viscerally trusted is to shine a light as much for ourselves as for the other. We are most loving of one another by being constant in our own growing. In saying yes to this vulnerable and dynamic level of being—living it ourselves and encouraging our heart's friend to live it also. We form a matrix of light and strength we can both rely on.

It is an experience of Spirit's invisible net of love in which we are held always. When our very cells trust Spirit's work within us it will not only have been yesterday, it will also be yes/today.

Embracing *All of It*

L ove is paradoxical. On the one hand we know each other deeply and on the other hand we know that we cannot really ever know the other completely. We live love by a continual repeated, mutual discovery of one another. Over and over in countless ways we find love for our heart's friend in small gestures of care and in the most ordinary details of connection. It is here that we learn to open to the context of the one we love.

A fish is not alive without water nor is a bird alive without air. As humans our air and water are the elements that have shaped us. We come to be our selves within the context of family, school, friends, interests, work and the landscapes we live in. We have a vast net of associations in which we are embedded--some wonderful and some that are fraught with terrible difficulty. Loving another in depth we must also embrace their context.

In the beginning of a friendship we may not realize that we are to be open to the whole field in which our friends have become who they are. Love asks us to embrace each other with all that made us and keeps us.

Embracing *all of it* is very difficult. We want to eliminate parts we don't like and add other parts. We want to determine what our mutual meaning should be. But all such efforts at control and manipulation will fail. Slowly we learn to let Spirit be the largest, mutual context.

ๅๅ

We are always engaged in the beloved or feared things of our past. They are part of us and seek love from us and love from someone whom we trust. All of it wants inclusion. We learn to care about the things that are meaningful to our heart's friends—the longed for things and the feared things. This is the context our friend is living. We can think of that context as ring setting for a jewel.

We support our friends to love what they already love. With no strings attached, we can be "for" one another. Embodying this willingness is never done. It must be lived daily. Neither is the process about some ultimate success, but about the humility that accepts failure and begins again and again.

Conscience

There is another meaningful way that deep friends love. Not only do we come to more consciousness together, we also come to conscience. Being aware is good in and of itself, but knowing that we know or shall we say knowing *with* (con sien cia) each other establishes us in a truth we cannot hide from.

We are not loved in a conscience way by many people or very often. How profound is the love that a person gives when he or she respectfully acts to further our conscience! Deep friends can call one another's deceptions and half lies. Where we often weasel out of knowing what we know alone, it's impossible to do so in the context of committed friendship. The truth is written in the heart and mind of our friend as well as in our own heart and mind. It becomes shared truth and a sacred trust.

There are so many layers to us humans, and those areas of shame and fear, of injury and distrust as well as the areas of soul beauty and competence are the very ones we protect and hide. Knowing that we know them, and knowing that our beloved friend also knows them, allows us access in a new way. We can bear their truth in all senses of that word.

Then it is not surprising that many companionships do not blossom into deep friendships because it takes such courage and responsibility to act as a loving conscience for and with another person in times of conflict and confused discernment. It is there so many feel deeply alone.

∞

As solemn as this mutual task is, we can be light about it all. Making fun of our selves or each other is that tickle-touch of humor that let's us be amused by our own ridiculousness, our habits of avoidance and subterfuge. Then what is heavy to bear can be brought to right proportion.

Laughter can be the recognition of the tragic and impossible seen from a startling angle, making it suddenly not only possible, but perhaps human, funny and even lovable.

In the throws of a great guffaw our tears run and our bellies dance. A big laugh is like a sob. We are crying and tickled pink at the same time. In laughter we are shaken free and so revivified into hopefulness and wholeness again.

Shared Work

It is by the shining interior light of our friendship that we illumine more than our own concerns. It follows that the love in a deep friendship naturally spills out into shared work in the world.

That does not mean that we do the same work necessarily, though it may sometimes be so. Rather we are supported by each other's journeys to give ourselves more fully to others in our particular way. The confluence of our shared enthusiasm and mutual interest to be of service becomes an energy field that allows us to explore and risk more. Learning with each other we find the courage to step over the invisible lines we draw in our native caution.

To take up our purpose in the world together is powerful. It is like gardening. Pruning, turning over new soil, feeding, and replanting are always present in life. As friends we will know what condition our soil is in, what it can bear, what it needs, what season it is in life and where support should be given. Through mutual awareness we participate in one another's work in the world and somehow it becomes shared work.

We help each other avoid many spiritual traps. One trap is feeling that we do things all by ourselves. We never do. Spirit is doing us all the time and often through the love of a friend. We will also avoid being possessive about accomplishments. We move from self-congratulation to the wonder of feeling that something has been done that is of value.

Our work in the world may be in the same place or in separate locations and about different concerns. Yet the harvest is communal. It feeds us both and many others. As deep friends we help each other garden our lives for the sheer privilege of doing so. We know that love is not something we do, but something we are given to be.

Knowing Nothing

To write about love is very difficult. We know so little about it, confusing need and fuzzy feelings for an experience that is both as familiar as the smell of our child's skin and as strange and invisible as the floor of the ocean. We know nothing really, and that is actually a comforting place to both begin and to continue. Knowing nothing we can relax and be present to learning. Knowing nothing is at least a truth we can embrace.

No doubt we will find how fickle we are when only feelings determine our way. Like New England weather feelings change continually. We love and yet often we disparage what we love. We are proud of those we love, and yet we seem to require that they be more than they can be or different than they are.

To love with any constancy and fullness of heart is not something we do, it is done in us by Love itself. Taken by surprise, even after years of loving someone or something, we find ourselves discovering them anew, as if for the first time. We surrender to something internal that is also externally there in living color. Deep friends actually love Spirit as they perceive it embodied in each other. It is felt by some people as a kind of recognition "from before" or "from forever and always". We know, yet have no way to know how and why we know it. That brings us full circle to knowing nothing yet feeling how Spirit is with us in conscience and confidence and shares the work of loving *all of it.*

ഝ

When we have the magic of knowing without knowing, we enter the world in participation instead of observation. It is like walking in a landscape and feeling it around us instead of flying over it in a plane or whizzing past it on a train. We escape our closed compartments, our sealed windows, and our habitual speed.

It is then we discover ourselves on sturdy ground where everything becomes both a self-discovery and an "us"-discovery. Then the held hand of the other is of such necessary beauty that we could never take it for granted. We would not know who was holding whose hand. In that shared landscape, if someone called us by Love's name we would both answer.

Last Word

To have a heart's friend and to be a heart's friend is to have a blessing and to be a blessing. I cannot think of a more sustaining way to grow in every way including spiritually. By such communion we become more than we could ever be alone. As Robert Louis Stevenson said, *a friend is a gift you give yourself.*

If, however, there is no one in your life presently that can serve in that capacity, please remember that Spirit is already there as your friend and accompanies you always. You can commune with Spirit and find that by listening with your heart you will hear, on an inner level, how Spirit holds you, guides you and loves you.

In a deep friendship we create a sanctuary where something dynamic can happen. It is a place of giving and receiving without strings, with no motivation to be "something" or "someone" —we simply offer ourselves in faith to one another. This giving has a quality of vulnerability and naked transparency. When such a gift of self is truly given and received, we meet as equals and are touched, confirmed, and enlarged.

Sheltered in the heart this way we stop searching and are found instead in the mystery of God who made us for life and for each other. There we experience a joy, which does not hesitate in the face of circumstance—be it uncertainty, suffering, fear or celebration—but rather encircles us and allows us to open to all we are.

How mysterious is Love.
It binds us close to one another
even as it gives us freely back to ourselves.

Acknowledgements

Thanks to Leslie Browning, my editor and publisher at Homebound Publications, for believing in this book and to Cynthia Bourgeault for so graciously writing the foreword. Thanks to my friend, Jan-Erik Guerth, editor at BlueBridge, for those wonderful conversations about true friendship.

This book would not be possible without my dear friends (you know who you are). As the Quaker saying goes "to listen a soul into disclosure and discovery is the greatest service one human being can offer another". It is what this book is all about and you have graced the way. Thanks to my dear family, of course. My gratitude also goes to my students and clients from whom I have learned so much about life and love. Finally I send a heart's song to Stanley, my partner, to whom this book is dedicated.

HOMEBOUND
PUBLICATIONS

AT HOMEBOUND PUBLICATIONS WE RECOGNIZE THE IMPOR-
TANCE of going home to gather from the stores of old wisdom to help nourish our lives in this modern era. We choose
to lend voice to those individuals who endeavor to translate
the old truths into new context and keep alive through the
written word ways of life that are now endangered. Our titles
introduce insights concerning mankind's present internal,
social and ecological dilemmas.

It is our intention at Homebound Publications to revive
contemplative storytelling. We publish full-length intro-
spective works of: non-fiction, essay collections, epic verse,
short story collections, journals, travel writing, and novels.
In our fiction titles our intention is to introduce new per-
spectives that will directly aid mankind in the trials we face
at present.

It is our belief that the stories humanity lives by give
both context and perspective to our lives. Some older stories, while well-known to the generations, no longer resonate
with the heart of the modern man nor do they address the
present situation we face individually and as a global village.
Homebound chooses titles that balance a reverence for the
old sensibilities; while at the same time presenting new per-
spectives by which to live.

CPSIA information can be obtained at www.ICGtesting.com
Printed in the USA
BVOW08*0746241013

334140BV00001B/1/P

9 781938 846106